SOY REALIDAD

SOY REALIDAD

Tomaž Šalamun

Co-translated by Michael Thomas Taren
and Tomaž Šalamun

Edited by Michael Thomas Taren

DALKEY ARCHIVE PRESS
Champaign / London / Dublin

Originally published in Slovenian as *Soy Realidad* by Založba Lipa, Koper, 1985

Copyright © 1985 by Tomaž Šalamun

Translation copyright © 2014 by Michael Thomas Taren and Tomaž Šalamun

First edition, 2014

Library of Congress Cataloging-in-Publication Data

Šalamun, Tomaž.
    [Soy realidad. English]
    Soy realidad / Tomaž Šalamun; co-translated by Michael Thomas Taren and Tomaž
    Šalamun; edited by Michael Thomas Taren. -- First edition.

    pages cm
    "Originally published in Slovenian as Soy realidad by Zaloba Lipa, Koper,
    1985"--Title page verso.
    ISBN 978-1-62897-088-3 (pbk. : alk. paper)
    1. Šalamun, Tomaž--Translations into English. I. Taren, Michael Thomas,
    translator. II. Šalamun, Tomaž, translator. III. Title.
    PG1919.29.A5S6913 2014
    891.8'415--dc23

                2014014009

Partially funded by the Illinois Arts Council, a state agency, and by the University of
Illinois at Urbana-Champaign.

This translation has been financially supported by JAK, the Slovenian Book Agency.

www.dalkeyarchive.com

Cover: design and composition by Mikhail Iliatov
Printed on permanent/durable acid-free paper

SOY REALIDAD

CONTENTS

CHILDHOOD MINE, PALM YOURS

Only there where there is no history, history
buries everything beneath itself.
I roar as I watch wounds in
the ribs of still unborned poets.

Hey dew!
Why don't you feel that I'm dew, too?
It's me.
The dew is fine.

And also, if I turn the clock
ahead and watch the grass and the earth
on my grave, for I always
enjoy my memories:

Where is what could
ruin our fraternity?

Hey dew!
Why don't you feel that I'm dew, too?
It's me.
The dew is fine.

THE CROSS

O wound!
The earth that sets asunder and swallows the time.
The frog with teeth that stings hills.
Ether, the dropping off in scales.
The scepter: ostrich's boulevard.

O dark sack of sand!
Memories that the mirror pushes under
the mattress so sheets wouldn't sing
and touch the waves of the pavement.
Do I really walk on the licked-off stone?

Why do questions pile up like bailiffs
They too have their sisters, children, people
and if a young doe pushes her snout under my armpit,
roses and strawberries ripen faster then
one round of mora: *tre! tre!*

Processes in nature are disposed like
our brain and our destiny.
The flour changes into the spinning wheel
and what is called arbitrariness
is the bridge of love: words extend the same way as
the penis, they grow like baby rabbits.
Mothers are afraid of storms,
still they don't drop from their teeth
their young ones while crossing the rivers.
We can beat the mind like Don Quixote,
but with it the knight's passion only increases.

O boats flung into my baskets
full of wolves.
Who in the Andes desires lobsters and from the field
demands a base made of blue buttons!
Who worships cathedrals only for the spires
and the fact that your belfries
are concealed from your being.

As if there were two towns: one on the earth
and one in the air, like the left and the right eye.

Four hits from the only blacksmith
and yet changes the heat, the genesis, the order.
Still aesthetes will torment themselves
with the original decanting over flesh,
still the palm trees will exhale fragrance.
Still there will be murdering of the insidious masses,
digged in the rear, into the dead sleeve of waters
demanding the explanation.
Why does the cow die if she drinks them?
Why does the bird die?
Why does the boat rot, even the cork on it
is not joyful, but black, greasy from the used
oil.

The sin piles up like a ziggurat,
and the ziggurat is designed also on the necklace
worn by the peacock.
Nobody can invent
the new atomic weight of love.

CANTINA IN QUERÉTARO

I see the horse shrieking when meeting the eyes
of another dead horse.
They're brothers, two angels with the apple,
the cataract of the underworld.
The sun on your mane is for you both.
Why are you tearing me apart, jealous colts?
Why do you stamp like janissaries?
Horses are sacred animals. You're both César Vallejo.
For not quantities flow through us, but spirit and
flame.
Is it possible the dead poet's genius
undoes into two rivers and tears in two like a handkerchief?
You're both one image and this is bread for millions.
Both my arms are the same length.
Both my legs are for all nations of the world.
My kiss is not a chain, look:
this is the pneuma breathed by Jakob Boehme,
it's virginal. I carry it in my breast
like a Karst woman carrying water in a pitcher on her head.
And if I have to listen again to these
petit bourgeois problems of Nicaean
councils and witness the liquidations
of our best tested guerilla cadre,
you, colts, will again go back,
route march to darkness. In this cantina
while others might stab you with knives,
I will calmly place small change
por mi copa de alma blanca.

DANGEROUS THOUGHTS

(Cavafy translated by Edmund Keeley & Philip Sherrard)

Said Francisco Macías Romero (a student
from Toluca in Querétaro, during
Šalamun's stay in Mexico in the second
half of the twentieth century of our era,
in part an Aztec, in part a Catholic:
"Strengthened by meditation and study,
I won't fear my passions like a coward;
I'll give my body to sensual pleasures,
to enjoyments I've dreamed of,
to the most audacious erotic desires,
to the lascivious impulses of my blood,
without being at all afraid, because when I wish—
and I'll have the will-power, strengthened
as I shall be by meditation and study—
when I wish, at critical moments I'll recover
my ascetic spirit as it was before."

QUERÉTARO

Who shrieks in the dew above the bank?
The red *noche buena* waits for a peacock.
Weary and sweet I tremble like a cypress.
It hurts.

Querétaro. Still the echoes from steps
among loud shrieks of birds at
sunset. White cloths on the tables and
vases of fruits. A biography of St. Paul,
dropped by us on the stony pavement.

THEY ALL

"They all love me here, servants
included. I'll wire you when I
know, Monday morning, after
nine. I'm scared. You stress too

much your s's. I'll take this sweatshirt,
your wedding one. I'll wait for
the next bus. Look, this is San Martin de
Pores, the small black man I was telling you

about. Is my scent nicer than your cat
with white ribbon? I'm not an angel,
I'm a man who wants to experience
that experienced by the one who gave us life.

I'm one of seven. My father is
three years younger than you. After I leave
you should fall asleep, so your heart doesn't
betray you and you don't lose your wife."

POPPY

Cover the people when I step in the area.
Throw on them blankets, tents, and powdered milk.
Dig them into the earth, I am a hamster.
Wrap them in a gauze.

Draw crosses on their mouths.
In Biblioteca Lorenziana there's a fire.
Breathe bread and earth and rain,
suffocate your kids with oat bran.

My soul is the dark vigilant agave.
The panther that breaks every cage.
When I march on the stars, my creation,
the white dust creaks under me.

FULL MOON

How sweet to meet the childlike soul resting in God!
Eyeballs, lakes, and black hair as a beast might have.
The neck you can hold better than a steering wheel
and the laugh the cannibals laughed that I saw in
a movie when I was little. And your scent is real,
Michelangelo's slaves are not as fragrant as you, Francisco.
You shouldn't cry, I cry. Look, even so, everything
hangs by a tiny hair. How could I explain this to any reasonable
being and to your mom. Do you really think you're not
handsome, ashamed to watch yourself
in the mirror? Stop carrying your comb so primitively
in your pocket. You breathe like bloom and
rower. I like everything you like.
I've never made love listening to Tchaikovsky.
Que te pasa niño!
How do you make it so the air crunches and rustles
for us both, and fall asleep like a dew,
so we swim and in the morning you tell me
your dreams and they confirm
you were truly there where I had been.

EL GRITO

Blood among divers.
Salt animals breathe.
You have mustaches and yet didn't fall off.
Your soul blots oaks.
You're a blossom and ripen by antenna.

Flowers ache, sleep aches.
Breathing aches and drops into lust.
Beer cups are crystal
in the violet Christ's coat.
Sheets no longer smell of the earth.

Pull off my gaze, Completion!
Why can I not behold the dreadful
secrecy crawling after me
like a shadow through Hades
with a dead infant in his lap.

Fill my nostrils with dirt.
Bread, wash the sleep of the righteous.
Tufts of leaves of grass, drum.
Let mana end defusing in my throat,
that I'll burn air.

THE MORNING

Birds warble.
What did stars do in the sky,
bump each other?
I dreamt saints had
yellow butter in their ears like us.
But then those sticks with the cotton didn't
exist yet, how long it took for them to clean themselves.
Sometimes all their lives.
I forgot a bit about you, kitty.
Don't worry, you're getting the cheese.
Coats lie on the floor.
Whose are these coats?
The wind comes not till two or three o'clock.

THE LITTLE MAN

The little man in mottled socks
walked the avenue and stepped on coffee.
Coffee is expensive here, stupid!
Why don't you go a bit further.

ABOUT THE MOUTH OF A RIVER

Rabbit, a gray tiny rabbit, why don't you put on weight?
Who likes you, pump! Your ears are scrolls
of bread, what can I do with them? Even if I
put them back on the horse, they fall down.

Rabbit, a gray tiny rabbit, I do best to throw
you in water, to soak your head with a daisy.
You violate my philistines, as you once more put
cabbage on the menu. My cabbage is sacred,
yours not. You eat it with your little teeth, but
your teeth don't multiply and replenish the earth!

Rabbit, a gray tiny rabbit, step on blue
paper, so your paws can be seen.
They're humble like orchids. I'm a lion.

PENSAMIENTOS: FRANCISCO'S FIRST POEM

Despierta ya soñador empedernido
de tu sopor ingenuo.
Vive tu realidad,
es tan bello soñar la realidad
sentir en tus celulas
la vida plena que lo Divino te ha donado.

No quiero que de mis palabras
brote alguna cizaña.
Anhelo dar vida a mis emociones,
gozar con mis ideas
materializar nuestras ilusiones.

Vivir y dejar vivir.
Volar, dejando volar.
La muerte no existe, llamemosle
SUEÑO DE PAZ.

El rio de la vida
brota en un instante
su caudal ahoga nuestro amor
por siempre.

En mis manos
conservo, mantengo
tu calor.
Las rosas marchitas de los siglos
te envuelven y tu las revives.

Mis labios se abren
para decir AMOR.
Mis actos son una manifestacion
de lo que pienso.

No soy un angel,
soy un humano que quiere
alcanzar la divinidad
de aquel Dios
que nos a dado la vida.

Soy, pués
un cimiento de mi mensaje.
Soy realidad.

SIERRA NEVADA

All history is in my body hair, every
bloody red atlas.
My body hair sets the cosmos to delight.
If a flower blooms, it blooms only
because I give it access to my body hair.
It's of granite, purer than heaven's tears
dropping on Hermes's chest.
And when little dogs have kids and give
birth to them: because of my body hair.
Because of my body hair Rome collapsed,
it was entangled.
On the sun, view of the Sierra, ants,
and trees and anthems, alloyed in zigzag.
Honey scratches my throat: my body hair.
Little horses change into bundles.
Ha! Who drew the back of the stone and
displayed the mountains precisely as they stand,
drew walls onto them and poured air over everything.
The world is a cake.
The heart, glaziness and almonds in it.
A body hair is more splendid than alcohol.
Jets graze together with sheep and goatlings,
elastic is the bridge from where the kings were thrown.
I rock.
My body hair is torrents.
Sometimes I bind the trunks with a thin wire
and attach them to the cart.
A little train puffing heavily like a pilgrim.
Get it done! I whisper blessed, history gets
more and more fragrant blooms.
I attract women because they have less body hair.
They're cold, wind blows on their head without a man
and kids are hunting for their father, their real

father, the one who puts his body hair in their
mouths, so that they can swallow thin,
polished hits of pool balls,
manna that bleaches their eyelashes.
I'm the body hair.
I'm the body hair's father.
I'm the chicken's little thighs on my
sheets, on which the wildness breathes,
inviting me with it's every breath
into bloom.

FOR THE SQUEAKER

When I die, hands of everyone
will shake terribly and
candles will shudder so hard
all my clothes and my
hand will be stained.
The riders will approach
from the left side.

TSAR NIKOLAJ

Numen and libido, the two green cups full of compote.
Look at the tiger, crawling in the black
briefcase.
Horses are soot.
Princess of Navarre changes her umbrella.
She'll send it to Europe.
There, behind the counter, the decadents stand,
standing upright they polish their diamonds.
The sunset, the end of the stock market.
We stuff honey pots into the mouths of giraffes.
There is a leaflet in one:
"Tsar Nikolaj should die!"

But before all of this we have to describe all his
cordage and twines. He doesn't have
handsome ears, his mustaches are too long.
Color of his hair, unimpressive,
the skin is not wrinkled.
would he breathe through his eyes
if we plug his nose?
He won't, my children, he won't.

IN FAREWELL

Shakuntala received the gifts from:
grass,
gazelles,
bushes,
rivers and ponds,
lilies,
(elephants gimped to watch this)
and the son of the moon's king.

RAIN

It rained during the night.
Did the snails sleep or paddle?
The pine tree strained itself and grew for a millimeter
and there, far away, Lebanon was bombed.

NO JOKES IN LOVE

Knitting needles are tired of gold.
I'd crawl on every corner.
In winter I'll wear a fur cap
to be warm in our lands
and teach rabbits to walk like
turtles.

SWALLOW THE MARBLES THEN!

Throw down that chalkboard, I need the bed cover!
You too will be packed in my leather
note pad, just be silent, please!
Aesop had a cask of wine in his belly.
The snakes swam in the cask of wine.
So he said to comrade Marjanca:
"If you make the planks loose,
not only make the planks
loose, but also make the iron
hoops swish out without
hurting me, I'll buy you a roasted
duck."
And the river melted so fast
it just lifted the ice breakers.
Children came to school
with the reddened cheeks.

COMIDA CORRIDA

My heart draws stars in the sky.
Blood is my rising pillar.
The sun scorches
the azul counter, while I'm walking
in the horseshoe, in U, cooking.
Night will come and I'll be tired.
I'll fall asleep and open the drawer,
so my soul will fly and
fliotz! schpliask! in the dense,
swelled muteness.
There, are the silver sticks that play with
breath on waves,
giving power.

THE KISS ACROSS THE OCEAN

O my birdie, how tired I am.
Do you want to see what I have written today?
By now I have the whole factory
and the mannikins dressed in little sacks.
I hung them on my thread
and glued them to the wall of the abyss.
They don't have ground under their feet,
they tug me constantly. Fooey, with
what rusty shovels they want
to be brave! I don't let them. Uhuh.
No. First you clean your shovels.
I take care of everything. The kitty
too. And I curse this too long arc
between letter and letter.
I know. Now some five of them ruffle
in the air or they roll in
Correo Central.
Why can't you puff like me,
look, the aspirated K
and now, now your body melts
like crumbs of bread on butter
and you fall asleep beautifully.

TOOF TOOF: ARC

Hungry bird from Samarkand
chews the putrid leaves.
What's up, honey?
Nobody cuddles you?
In Chihuahua, I've seen such a train,
that I carried it on my chest.
And if I roll you into my trunk
and carry you more southward,
will you be in worse repute?
We'll do like this, birdie.
I'll put dressing on my salad
and tuck you into my backpack,
as birds cannot travel by train.
There I'll provide you so many worms
you'll squint your eyes.
And then you'll fly away again,
fat, so strong, and able
to break the window pane.

GRASSES

I broke my oar.
Seven floors, seven upholstered
dining rooms, seven apertures
for cooking collapsed
under my rolling pin.
Why?

The trumpet with ground toad in it
and a cube of sugar in the gas tank, so I burn
more sweetly.
Why can I not burn through?
Why does it return me to my knees,
on tigers skins from where I beckon cameramen.
Why is the tunnel snuffed!

Pariahs! Saint Ursulas! Kronenbergs!
Do you recall? You didn't sleep.
You hemmed my white breeches for first communion.
The maize brush decided everything.

An ink nose, piebalded weed,
Ulysses with such muscles that he by himself
was able to grip the beam, the battering ram, by which
the castle fell.
And if I dirtied my hands, I
withdrew, caressing the unborns in my belly.
Let them be born blind, scabby.

Do you know what the Scarlet Bull
stamp of eighty centavos means?
Do you know how they hunt
the heralds of spring?

Do you know how the most innocent
willows are used for baskets?

Roosters are put on pretzels, they wet them.
When the pretzel is puffed up and the rooster
almost dies, they burn him at last.
Who holds in the second act of my suicide?
Why lock it in the family album?
I swam seven rivers.
Seven times picked grapes in Champagne.

And the rider who rushes the broadness
of the spring, don't you see he's on sleds?
They always film me only up to my ankles,
so the luster of my galleys gets lost.
Where does it go!
Who drinks my milk before it hits my mouth?
Are you a frog? Are you a plant? Are you a crystal ball?
Do you have a lucky pinkie?

I saw. You used your own brain
for gluing stamps.
Boca negra, fat rolled into your coat.
Why does the slot hiss?

The army marches,
one day you'll fall, my rider.
And in the eternity nothing will be left after you.
You'll leave your eyes and your luster on
these grounds, as we all—The Others—who were your
Loyal shadows.

OPUS DEI

What touches me is consecrated.
That's right! Even
hard licking and lazing under the shower won't do.

Did you ever die without the air?
I did.

Were your eyeballs ever wrapped in
azure paper strips?
Mine were.

I ate up every alley tree.
Poured the Forbidden City into myself.

For you remain clear steps,
beams of nature and caresses of the sun.

I give you back the measure of man.

SEED

I know, the fold is theophany
and my fingers,
the dead hungry does.
When will the blossom die?
When will the water carry me from the shores?
When will the pulsing of my veins
be only a phantom in the vase?
I know, I'm the memory of heaven,
the dust to which the poem
kneels.

THE AZTEC

Lilies are mystery,
wild little boar!
With the skull which will break
like the skull of the otter. And like
the sun's scissors tiring my flowers.
Like this rumbling of the engine which
goes as long as it goes. Why are you
born into the red air, fluid!

The birth is the collapse of a bridge.
The last black cat's fur falls out.
And my palate, the teeth and the tongue,
Komna, where I was skiing,
are all signed in for death.

Who keeps repeating the damp treacherous
seed, no more than
cramps of the blackest karmas.
White otter, look!
Clouds ruin themselves in front of your eyes
but they don't shred the fairytale.

What should the rabbit's ear do with my saliva!
I won't console him, even if screaming:
No me muerdas!
Muerde me!

FRANCISCO'S SECOND POEM

Huir en mil suspiros.
Ahogar en multitud de sollozos.
una voz que impregna implacable
la sed de justizia.
Una letra no basta para
decir lo que siento,
mucho menos una palabra.
Lo que necesito es un
cumulo de frases que te digan
cada uno por lo que sufro.
El nombre prohibido,
el señuelo inmortal de
fragilidad recondita
es indispensable para
detener tu carrera.
Pero donde encontrarlo?

No se, debe haber un lugar,
pero tu sigues trotando, y asi
alegrando la vida de aquellosque te necesitamos.

DEATH'S WINDOW

To stop the blood of flowers and to reverse the order.
To die in the river, to die in the river.
To hear the heart of the rat. There's no difference
between the moon's and my tribe's silver.

To rake the field and run to the edge of the earth.
To carry in the chest the crystal: the word. At the door
the soap evaporates, the fire lights the day.
To turn around, to turn around once more.

And to strip the frock. The poppy has bitten the sky.
To walk empty roads and drink shadows.
To feel the oak where there's the mouth of the well.

To stop the blood of flowers, to stop the blood of flowers.
Altars stare at each other, eye to eye.
To lie down on a blue cabbage.

FOR YOU ALL

Mexico is my Pentecost.
The snake warming herself in the sun
at the hour, when mankind sleeps.
Crawl, snake, lie down, snake,
kill animals and strangle them!
Save what you can.
There's no crumb of bread or ear of puma
that doesn't deserve to be saved.
Nowhere is written part of the earth should
freeze.
For what is bewitched into ice will
grow.
For what is crushed into cynicism and
flabbiness will again bend its
grids.
Mexico is my Pentecost.
For you all.

THE TURTLE

The turtle, with her poison
geography and hard shell
can alone breast-feed the star.
The star where soy grows
in parallel green skies,
while every soldier in the world
swallows his saliva and cannot
swallow it.

The turtle with her dreadful
dynamite and the veil like
a pair! a pair!
restores the mother
from dry milk
rolled over by tanks.

The turtle alone with her sly
head and watery sounds
—the earth's back rolls over—
kills and holds back
death so the cake in the mouth
shudders and gives birth.

The cross can be peeled off,
and He won't be aware.

Only the turtle vomits memory.

Estoy entre coplas escribiendo esta carta.

Es necesario decir algo, para saber que estoy vivo.

Lo unico que viene a mi mente es tu nombre.

Creo que estoy solo, pero recapacito y me doy cuenta
que tu pensamiento es el que me acompaña.

He hecho muchos amigos en esta tierra, pero ellos
tienem otras misiones y aunque quisieren
acompañarme no podrian.

Se ahogan en mis cabellos los suspiros de un corazon
que sufre sin saber porqué.

El sonido apegado de las canciones llega a hasta aquí,
quieriendo con su ritmo hacerme sentir con ganas
de bailar y de centar pero no puedo. Estoy inmovil,
no quiero dejar de escribir estas lineas, quiero
morir estampando letras y una terrible comezon me
carcome los huesos.

Oh! Si pudieran verme. Estoy solo.

Mi pecho se descubre al amparo de una risoria lámpara
de azufre; perdon, dije azufre... He querido decir
petróleo.

Será que ya no estoy en este mundo?

Lo que sea. No quiero seguir pensando en más cosas,
los techos no han tenido nunca pensamientos y por
eso todavia siguen existiendo.

Mis sueños azules se desvanecen.

El olor café de la mierda acaricia mis seines sin poder
siquiera olfaearlo un momento.

No es cruel senti ahora a la dulce caricia tus manos
mojadas.

No puedo ser, tus labios me han besado, tus ojos me
han mirado.

El rancor del otro día lo he olvidado, me emborrache
tanto de recuerdos, que estoy impotente ante la luz

encarnada de un sexo indecifrable.

No ahora no quiero pan, tal vez mañana cuando todo
este terminado queda tener la tranquilidad de
probar bocando.

Más no se si lo que ahora pienso, lo que ahora repito en
este mismo instante quede encantado y tu amada
belleza se vea terminada en unas cuantas cenizas.

Es por eso que me estoy acabando, es pore so que sigo
escribiendo. Por ti!

THE SKY ABOVE QUERÉTARO

Who are the beings snuffing in the black sky
starting to smell like rat kings?
Beads tinkle in flowerpots
and the rose would jump like a frog
if she weren't pinned.
Are stars the burden?
Is not water the fruit of billions and billions of years?
Crystals don't change.
You don't catch a rabbit with your hand.
And the plaster from the cathedral fell on
the ice cream vendor's handcart.

Who are the beings stopping my
pace to make the leaves rustle?
The keys hung on ropes of dew
begin to clink.
Does the king of rats himself now want to trap
me with symbols and hours?
My handcart doesn't have a beard.
Stony plates of my tables
decay like Conquista.
And again in the sky an orange appears,
I spin it with a swift and religious
gesture
so the stalk strains and shucks off and—

does the earth breathe then?

MINOS

The heart, who is the power and the might of the earth,
blows away the snow and the sheets.
The birds fall like
white balls like dashing onions.

For does not there exist no more
patient and persistent
being than the Minotaur,
measuring every arc,
every step,
every home,
for just one pivot.

The heart, who is the power and the might of the earth,
saps even the sequoia
growing in my garden.

Only in its fall
is this silken image,
the final whiteness
of teeth grown together
which feeds my soul with its
death.

TO DEAF BROTHERS

I got tired of your bland heaven.
Foot to foot, mouth to mouth, you dead ones.
The blossoming choked? By what might?
Gulag in your toady heads spreading like cancer?
I carry God in my heart, I make a present of him
like water for those who haven't had it.
Who languish upon imaginary provincial
tectonics, upon the pedestal of suicide,
our national champion.
Who totter, kill, sleep,
who don't feel fear.
I refuse to be free in every place
to then fall back in empty dry
blackness only in my native country.
I'm not a cynic, I'm a poet, a prophet.
With my life I go there where I am.
I won't be strangled by your nets,
your Saint-Beuvish mumblings are
criteria for no one.
I won't stagger and fall like Cankar.
They won't gold plate me with gold
into a sterile ritual like Župančič.
My element is the sea, if you don't have it,
I give you it.
My element is the air, killed and poisoned,
now cleansed.
If I'm the only one in whom freedom breaths,
I won't surrender.
Rather death than this humiliating genocide of your
marmalade.
The soul is eternal, you didn't know.
I have told you.
This place will survive with all our terrible

strain. All of us.
And if you stumble clumsily under my feet,
I'll kick you around like ants.
Rather one alive, witness to his grace
and excruciations than this glued Hades's
gelatin, not even a shadow of a trace
of alive people and noble
time, that breaths also under this earth,
above these heavens, you need only
fangs, teeth to strike with the bliss of gods
at the heart of this
downcast destiny, so someone
wakes up and hears.

Gracias a la vida, que me ha dado tanto.

ABOUT HEAVEN AND EARTH

In the post-Šalamunian period,
in the year of our Lord three,
while cooking chicken as per Metka's
instructions, to save a little, and
to need not go to the earth
too soon;
I watch the sunset and tell
myself: I know,
the sun is in my chest.
What will they do
if I don't give it back.
Better throw this counting
in their head.
Call the number, the taxi will
take you to the plane.

THE NAME OF THE WORLD

My name doesn't come as an angel,
but as a comet cutting the sky.
Flowers in the vase
in the night
are thrusted in
the middle of the day and
the udder becomes more
salty and more smarting to the calf.
Birds repeat their brainless behavior,
they frot the leaves of the tree and take
off in flocks of panic. Do they
fly toward heaven?
No.
Heaven is the cut at through stone.
Skin, the burning wood, it
has to burn till it's burnt through,
the curtains hiding the nature of
God are torn off. It
is possible to wipe the youngster's
nose if you stretch out and
want to. Why does this lady think
events pursue her and
becomes restless if the light starts
shining above time and space?
Breathe calmly.
Not a hair will be bent.
My name breathes,
as it rains,
as the rivers run,
like animals shifting from hip to hip
as people die or come to life.

FLOWER'S GARMENTS

I've seen the flower growing from the sand.
What does this flower mean?
She had a saddle in her blossom.
What does this saddle mean?
When I rode the saddle fell away.
The sea remained and by the walls yellow
noodles. Some noodles rolled,
others halved themselves,
one saw Yellow without shape.
Water bloodied.
Leaves started to fall in.
What I smelled
I knew was laurel.
I started to sense the ground under my toes.
First the ground moved.
It seemed corroded and hard-backed.
I couldn't remember the turtle had carvings.
Water ran away.
Under me everything floating on water ran.
There was no ground.
I walked on the empty hardness.
Far away, a long, wet broom
slid across the horizon,
I did not know if it's alive or dead,
if the thing the broom wrapped was legs
or chest hair, or just something hanged on it
and it might not even be a broom.
Then all of us were sucked into a soft matter,
a boiling mirror, but it didn't hurt.
It was boiling only because it was a liquid
and not a hot thing, and it started to harden up.
I was in the flower growing in sand, up to my waist,
and I knew I could now go anywhere I wanted.

I DOGEAR THE SURFACE OF WATER
WHERE THE HOLY SPIRIT ALREADY EXISTS

Blood that flowed on my body
at First Communion went into
tunnels and from the tunnels into
daylight.
It slipped over a platform and
wetted the head of a snake.
The snake didn't like red
so it changed into
a seal.
My blood I changed into water
to keep him alive.

NIHIL EST IN INTELECTU . . .

Here's how I recognize God:
a ripe pear in the mouth or
that silken explosion of air
breaking in bursting empty
blueness.
Head, hair are washed instantly.
I fear that—
let's say your eyes—
will drip onto my hands,
will let scent toward the sky or
tumble to the underworld like
Savica Falls.
And always I hear a fluttering of flags,
elegant crackles as if of the sinking
Titanic or a hen torn
apart.
And if all this happens:
I *give* the seal!
I give back the endless virginity.
For the sad ones are only
those who were never ripped apart.
Sí, que te veo como un Dios, Hombre!

EVENING, AMONG MUSES

Mouse! My grandchild, my suitor!
At sunset I see your two white little
eyes and in them
two baskets of red flowers.
Who will drink wine of pressed
cyclamens! Aren't you afraid, Father, you will
ruin the shape of the basket and the juice
of your eyes will spread?
Mouse! My grandchild, my suitor!
Your belly is the skin of the dead rabbit,
crucified above the Parthenon.
Or above, brothers, the World Trade Center,
because rain falls to earth always from
below. From the sea.
And my grandchild, whom I beat with my
racquet so he falls in even harder spurts
toward the Statue of Liberty,
my suitor, dies in the air.
His eyes melt
and unbolt the door for the scent's
free way to heaven.

NOCHE BUENA

How many spans of my sperm already dropped on my
homeland? Do you have to trudge? Was Christmas
beautiful? I'm worried about your boots, are they
warm enough? I have ones Echeverria wore. While
skiing, please, don't hem too much. Fresh snow
is the most tender and don't forget in the crystals
there are still the necks of my little ones, alive. Did you
go to midnight mass? Did you hear my jingle?
I saw the black bird bashing around a vault. Carriages
waiting outside. Here the Pacific had hugely foamed and
the whole country got covered by red flowers growing
for the Holy Night. I cried in the churches,
Christ cries no more. Heads of saints fell off and
smashed the glassy cages. My voice smashed them.

TO THE HEART

Raucous black sky, why did you swallow my
proof?
Who authorizes this gluttony?
My brothers are flowers.
Can you still smell haystacks and lemons blooming?
The body, dipped in water, loses its scent.
Kids on the coasts smoke their pipes.
We jointly burn our eyelashes.
Raucous black sky, did you tally the food?
What do you do in a crowd with white cherries?
Is there any wedge in your gluttonous cave?
What kind of papers do you burn under the pagoda?
Don't birds crash into your eyebrows?
You, who can't divide the yolk from the white,
where do you keep your colors?
You think I'll feed you like an hourglass
that can be rotated into eternity?
I'll break the horseshoe, we'll see if you go on
breathing!
And your barriers will burn down
under the water's surface.
Raucous black sky, my intimate!
Show, show the stones.
Let the otters' eyes on them be pulverized
so you'll count and sniff better.
You're the belt!
No-father!
Your procession of clayey and silky flags
goes mad at the touch of each other.
Where then is the papier-mâché?
Do the stars get hurt in my body?
Have you ever asked them?
You have your gods shut in bowls like peasants

their cabbage trod down in barrels.
You're deaf!
I've bitten off your heel, five times!
But it grows back like the beard of saints in the deserts
and they don't eat at all.
The earth is my bonbon, glutton!
The rest of the fruit we'll go halfs.
I beat the carpet dust in your mouth
to make you cough, black one!
And my children, I'll roll them
and I'll bend and I'll glue them so they'll leap up
and cut your throat while you smack and dream
about warmth as you drink my blood.
Raucous black sky, give me back my number!
Do you see these damp curved paws?
They're yours if you agree to the rules of the game.
Melancholy should flow like a river through us both!

DECEMBER 8, 1980

170 YEARS AFTER GÉRARD DE NERVA'L MOTHER'S DEATH

Dreadful monotonous tobacco plantations!
Where is mama, where is some chair?
In the flesh of El Desdichado no more Nerval.
He was killed by the bell's tolling
and curls pouring from the
floor upstairs.
Bugs are imbecile.
They tramp in the black corridors chiseled
by the race of the fresh.
Everyone not shutting taps will die!
Hoops have no body.
Today 170 years have passed since Marie-Antoinette-
Marguerite Laurent was buried
at the Polish Catholic
cemetery in Paris.
*Elle n'était qu'une fille d'un marchand
linger!*
Therefore, exactly at this moment—
on the other continent, at Alameda—
my body walls burst.
I'll ransom you, Gérard!
Because you, the unweaned child,
weren't even aware.
I'm fisically experiencing her death.

"Černič?"
"Didn't meet him. He's accused of the denunciation."
And archimandrites, in the beep between white and white,
copy the juicy, secret, glimming bonds. The mucus
staggers in precisely premeditated muggled composures and
misshapen stings, duped in silent bora, they protect the little hand.
Did he kill a cow or a cow's shadow?
Did he rock the foundation and stain it with milk in the
belly's cortex?
You'll never smash the rings behind the altar with the hammer.
Nutrition. Mom's kamikaze.
Barbed wire *die Rumpelkammer*, the prodigious *Carlina acaulis*.
The tablets.
Moses's shoulders in the archer's eye.
Flan! Flan! Flan!
The trench becomes longer and longer.
Will the godfather with the red spiked boots help?
Will he shelter the wild boar against the soul's little cap?
After-boats are always dried-up cups and what turns
around the So-Called, is always turned around with his bare feet.
Here-I-Stand, yes.
Falling I call the whore, named plant.
It buds octaves, never body hair.
Whistles are not tatooed nor covered by a sack,
lurking behind the cyclostyle.
Listen, heart!
Agave is a seal, a brass blowed up like a fire of
misfortune between beaming gums of saints, not knowing
if her name is emptiness, beaming, black, monkey-like or
the murder of tits.
Down the flesh path . . .

THE PHOENICIAN

I have yet the pheasant's radiant red
strings in my mouth.
The heart of the puppet doesn't bleed,
the tail bleeds.
Why do you use the nob?
Are the jobless less useful?
Will capital clean windowpanes?
Will magma sizzle the silence in the cavity?
Let the dormouse escape in the forehead of the sunset.
Let the city grab its reins.
Let fornicators line their bones with cork,
they'll catch fire sooner!
And *otchi tcharnaje* . . .
This time, there will be no milk after the paleolithic.
Wreaths shut in butter, shut in a glassy
casket in the hydra's snout under the tree-tooth,
left shadow, microbes, blown up by
Job, flushed tender shivering gelatinous
Law morphing into soccage.
At this early hour, brothers?
Don't you surpass yourselves with these mining projects?
Don't your stakes have their own bones?
And why not!
Are there no mines on the fields yet?

The bifurcation:
1. The nature under the tooth is different than
the nature under the toes.
2. The nature under the tooth is the same as the nature
prostitute.

You roll your carpets at the wrong ends, reconnaissance team,
seeing no clear chaos through the racquet, stiffy!
Cut off the magnet to the bull of the epic poem!
And enter the wooden door, not the black,
the sand doesn't burn.

Utter this:
turbans are poured over by boiling sap
and the language is glued as an aluminum strip
to the bitumen in frogs.

I am her belly.

NORTHERN SEAS

Don Rodriguez, kill the dog!
He stepped on your bread, don't you know?
Don Rodriguez, kill the dog!
He crumpled your green sail.
Don Rodriguez, kill the dog!
I repeat for the third time!
For, if his mouth grows up together with the sea,
we'll lose the way,
loitering on the shores during cold nights
and Olson's glasses,
the trap for all us tailors and sailors
will pierce.
We'll never be hops again
and drink each other.

ROBI

Sometimes, in the night, when everybody is
asleep, I cry. I know I'll go to hell.
Aunt Lisa won't go, and she's fatter than me.
Pillows prickle me.
I cannot sleep because I think too much.
When I'm not crying, I turn on the bulb.
Only if I make a rabbit with my hand
so that he goes on the wall, I get calm.
I have no friends as I fell from the steps
when I was three years old.
They say I was so scared that
I'm falling apart even now.
They call me Trashcan.
My dad works all day long.
My mom works at the Price Shopper.
Lisa cooks and beats me because she doesn't find a husband.
In school everybody is thin.
We have a school with a crumbling wall.
The fence is all rusty and if you
grab it you get brown hands.
I always wipe up my brown hands in the grass
so that the brown color doesn't get on my pants.
No one picks me up at school anymore.
When I grow up I'll be all alone.
Aunt Lisa is stingy like a skunk, she saves for her dowry,
she never gives on my plate enough food that I need.
I don't eat anything.
Stars must be very light.
Sparrows are not as light as I thought,
I weighed them.
For their size they're as heavy as me.
If I could fly I'd lose weight.
I know how the air rubs on your cheeks if the window

in the car is open.
Only my legs are normal.
Now I speak what I think.
Who does not speak what he thinks, falls apart.
Huge animals grow inside him and press
his belly with their backs.
Sometimes I think I'm a box where
there is
another Robi.
And that in that Robi there is a third Robi.
That each of us goes in all directions all alone.
Once I'll release both of them.
I'll buy a very thin rope and tie both of them on their
legs, so they'll pasture their way on their own.
I'll be without them all day, all night and if
my belly gets smaller, I will cut the rope
and they'll get lost in the space where they pasture.
They say: if someone truly wants to lose his weight
he should not eat for a week.
But if I'd leave them outside for a week, they
might freeze.
They might get lost.
It's not for sure I'd get thinner if they didn't exist.
Not for sure.
And it would look like I even don't have arms.
It's true.
They're both my arms and my brother, I have one
on both of my shoulders and it's 'cause that they're
inside my body is like having wings
of the butterfly in the chrysalis.
One day they'll go out.
That day my arms will dry up.
I'll throw my old two arms in hell,
I'll walk the steps and singe them.
I don't have other brothers, Aldo is blond.
It cannot be: one brother blond the other black.

I'd like to go to the mass alone by myself, not together.
Aldo should hit into the church door and
remain mashed there like a lump of snow.
They should all remain mashed there.
There shouldn't be any squeezing in the church,
you should be able to stare into God's eyes.
But now the people bring in the church the stench from
the kitchen.
It doesn't help if they dress well, it doesn't help,
I smell food.
I smell food at the elevation.
I smell food at the confession.
They don't allow me to touch Jesus.
Once they allowed people to kiss his
legs, but now they want to draw him as
a gym teacher and that's disgusting.
Aunt Lisa is the most disgusting, she's
the fattest, and that's why she doesn't find a husband.
I'll pull out the fence at the school.
And when my mom comes home she won't
have those dead eyes.
And my daddy will read books to me.
The story about the grain.
Why am I the smallest and the most fat?
Why do also rabbits mate?
Couldn't God at least make that rabbits
were pure who are not guilty of anything?
Everything alive that grows up mates and the sinning
at the outskirts of deserts devours incessantly.
Bushes.
Grass.
It dries even those little pools known only to the
Arabs.
People mate and their eyes go out.
The soul flows away from a man already when young
like the wine from the bottle held by a drunkard

who cannot even find his mouth.
I'm fat because I'm withdrawing my soul.
I withdraw it for all three of us.
Robi, Robi, Robi, Trashcan, Lump.
It's better to go to hell with your soul than to go to
heaven if you have to get rid of everything.
I'll pull out that fence even if my pants
turn brown as shit.
Pillows prickle me.
They turned off my bulb.
They say I'm not sleeping if my bulb is turned on
but it's the other way around.
If the light is on I calm myself 'cause I can see my
rabbit.
If I see my rabbit I can pray for him.
I can pray for every part of his body,
for ears, for paws, for his gray belly, for his
eyes, for letting him have calm eyes.
If I pray like this for awhile and move my hand
very slowly, my hand becomes the rabbit.
Sometimes the rabbit is totally on the wall,
sometimes he's completely in my hand.
Pillows prickle me.
The window must be open but it should be
warm anyway.
They shouldn't close it, you could suffocate,
but the air should not go around too much either.
The air that goes around too much mates.
Everyone that mates loses his independence.
The air also dilutes like old sugar that
has lost its strength
The air should be always be fresh, but inside, in the soul,
the air should only go around in the soul.
I'll cut wounds into myself.
Let the rose grow from my wounds so my rabbit
has company.

And below the rose it should be such a carpet of clover, like it is at the Bay of Ankaran.

OPUS

I'm a stone.
The bottom of the pain shined on by the moon,
by the sun not. I'm the train, undone,
people don't greet me anymore from their fences.
I'm hay set on fire
to arouse your hunger.
The attentiveness is erased.
I'm smoke,
the torn-apart circle of smoke, bluer than plankton
devouring the color of the sea, though it glitters.
I have a crushed chest.
Horses are walled in.
The river, unsticked from water
dries up the riverbed that it used.
The seed, that grows, is a dead spell beyond the earth.
For where there is the trunk of an oak tree
there cannot be tender fogs and
swaying of maple leaves.
The carpet in the drawing room is red.
And the noble color of parquet slats is brutally
hidden with the artifacts of the human hand.
There is blood of slaughtered sheep,
therefore we walk softly on them,
till we're choked by the breathing of their
lives.

FOR DAVID

It's evening.
The birds perch on the trees with a racket
and I think:
if I were my son,
would I too leaf through Larousse
before I started to talk?
Would it harm him?
Would he be amazed at this noise?
Would he ride a horse in the Sierras, young?
Tremble in front of the godlike shapes?
A green T-shirt,
a violet sweater,
the arc made by the incision between a pane
and a tin ledge—looked through a glass
of a fearsome craftsman, Maya—
on my patio?
Would Robert also visit him,
drink beer, tell how he
planted trees in the land
where it rains constantly and the Pacific
waves strike against rocks?
Does the soul extend with flesh?
Didn't the centaur keep his legs stretched out?
For if our scent leaves us,
how would the gods track us down,
they too are brittle fragile beings
like little ducks and our ancestors.

I'M CURSED.

Flowers dry up by me,
because I make love only with God.
My paws are washed by a cat.
Your insistence burns.

I don't swallow saliva, I swallow You,
who gave me life.
Will my heart blow up the noise?
We all die and go away.

The rain erases me.
Will loves burn in fire?
Will you catch sight of who you are
without me?

THE DEER'S FACE DOESN'T SMELL LIKE FLOWERS,

more like a blasting powder.
The flesh sea for just one oak.
The bell, your wet gum
dangles like hens
not noticed by the hawk,
not eluded by the deer.
Hops it even the bellman.

THE ARM THAT WALKS, KNEELS AND JUMPS,

will strangle our mass.
It shot our face
open.
The frog is a homesickness and a shaft.
The fruit will begin to vacillate and undo.
Woods, smelling lemons,
you're the treason.

GEORGES DE LA TOUR! GEORGES DE LA TOUR!

I see how you climb!
How you eavesdrop the hammering blacksmith
and peek at his watch.
I don't know if you break off your seal.
The beauty of the angel is in the cask
that bolted your heart.

SCENE

No. We collect wood. We tie up the Bible around
mice's waists. Bees rustle like a fifth column.
John, did you really go to Egypt by throwing beans out
in front of you? Texts say: you threw 'em, swam
in the air, bent down and had a sip of beer. There
you built your headquarters and turned the
pyramids downside up. Virgins grunted, on their
bellies the juice flew. The king carried a cloak
on a wire for a Dope. Back then nowadays's
ambassador didn't exist yet. So the sun thundered
twice: first when it jumped and second time
when it became a red tunic and covered religions.
And me with a toothpick poured schnapps in
their souls and today we have what we have.

ADAM HEAD

Wherefore a toad in my frying pan, screamed
our first lady. And why? Didn't I tell you I'll break
wood on your head if you didn't dry them
enough? You think we'll fuel your sweaty
back too? Of course, on what should our profiteer
lean against when there was no text yet. Adam was
blind. He still believed that Jordan was a tree;
that the sky was made of sacks; that a paper blows
from the North, but not from the South; that the
East is a great circle made of a fig that you should
put on your stomach if a snake bites you;
that shadow doesn't come from the sun, but from
donkeys; that hair is for drinking water; that the
Messiah will come who from a great distance will
smell myrtle; that birds are crumbs and crumbs
are kilims; and that the tree in paradise is a pear tree.
He's been hoodwinked to the bottom of godly mother
and even further. It's an apple tree, ass.

FALLS

In a billion steps we found pieces of glass wool.
Now this will be an inundation *Mira que suerte:*
conseguí una piernita igualita a la tuya. And the hero
Noah? The triumphal arches betrayed us already
the third thousand and seventieth time and we
didn't know if the pea is the slaughtered fir
and if we roasted the captive too heavily and if we
quickly pushed the hydraulic buttons to unhinge
the mountains, in short: it was about as chaos as
ultramarine. Even now planks screech. Even now
Windischers are pale. Camels still jostle and neither
their backs pass through their teeth nor the children
tears through the eye of the needle and Herod
cooks his new wine. Still today the sun sets and bees
gather honey, still today flowers break but lips don't.

PRAYER FOR BREAD

Who will not know how to drink the miracle, will
burn, it is so horrid. And who, in the miracle,
will not bulldoze the soil
will be like a wing abandoned by birds.
We're people, not flowers.
Their peace blooms from dead flesh,
let's not surpass the events.
The spirit never loses itself in haste
and if it sets itself in motion, empty, it comes
back. I'm a circle, until I become power,
and if I slash your face,
if I slap your shriek in your sleep,
if I keep disowning like I did before
as the poison of chaos, squat then like a sacred
animal just breast-fed.
Kiss the earth and throw the doom on me.
Chain me with your hate,
so I will crush you into
love.

GOD FROM THE EIGHTH FLOOR

In your lips is the life of the one
who gave life to me, too.
You're borrowed, traveler!
In your eyes are waterfalls I drink
and your hair has the fragrance of a good animal.
Don't cry, I won't snatch away.
I'm not me.
Don't shoot, you won't shoot yourself.
Do what I opened you for,
what you're kneeling for.
Pray in flesh.
You're a spring
and the white butterflies that flitter
above your naked dark skin—
wait! hear those sirens, do you think
there's a hold-up at the YMCA—
will become Tarzan
and Tarzan a big red tree.
I gave you milk, man!
Don't forget!

METKA

A piece of a living heart is not as flat
as a wafer, nor as white.
I'm watching limos through the glass.
O luck! *No más! No más!*
The most subtle springs live to see the day
when they'll be blessed with the saltiness of the sea.
And fish who need
enormous waters to be able to swim:
only in the mountains does snow melt.
From there the Holy Spirit only starts
to assemble, waiting for you,
the water who will guide him to the sea.

DAVID

If my son meets me,
how should he react?
Should he be scared?
Did Michelangelo really meet David?
Important is that he carved him.
For if you encircle him today,
sitting on the steps outside,
waiting with whom you will encircle him,
it still smells like Florence,
flowers,
Michelangelo.

THE BOY WITH A SMALL BUNDLE

In rubble, beneath the infinite roosters of bread,
dwelled the boy with a small bundle. She
loved him. On Sundays he went out. And when
he came to the bridge made of tiger's fur, titmice
were already sleeping. Does anyone live here?
he asked. Does anyone live here? he asked
again. There was no answer. He drank his crumbs
and milk and absorbed himself in thoughts.
Maybe the sun is the son of the devil. Maybe
animals love dough. Maybe in Spain slaves
and grasshoppers who like to race on camels
grow on trees. There're also people who
die without owning their house. And he
himself licked the tiger's fur and kept on walking.
And he came to the tower where there were
hens inside. O midges, he said, making a mistake,
how are you? And violet midges and hens
appeared on a mantle. The doorkeeper gave it
to him as a gift. And the boy didn't sleep
on the cauldron anymore, but on this soft gift.

CHRIST

If I'd eat my mom, the fish would tear her up
already in my throat. I'd better post her
on the gun. Let her flutter like a flag with wet paws,
thought the boy with the small bundle before
he fell asleep. For a long time he didn't dream at
all, then he suddenly saw Christ, how he eats kohlrabi.
Why do you do this? he sayeth. Why don't you leave
kohlrabi in peace? Christ didn't know what to do,
no one till now did reproach his greenery.
What should I eat, he said. We'll go hunting,
said the boy with the small bundle, for sure you'll
catch a rabbit. And they went. The light that
poured from Christ's belly diminished and they
started to stumble on stones. I'm not skilled, said the
Lord, I never caught a rabbit. Leave it to me,
said the boy with the small bundle, only
the light's missing. And Christ had eaten another
kohlrabi and the light was back immediately.
You cheat me, said the boy. The light should
shine by itself. The rabbit will be just for me if you
don't do better. And it was so light that rabbits
were like holidays. And one gave them his eye,
the other his nose and this was plenty and nobody died.

THE MARMALADE

And he wished for more marmalade than
he used to get in school. Gypsies practiced their
music. The schoolteacher threw blankets on them,
scolded them and called them *torremolinos*.
Gypsies just laughed their sweet laughs, they didn't
understand this word. There was also a gray
bird on the windowsill. I'll die soon, said
the boy to the bird. And the bird convoked
the bees and the bees said to the doe: we'll
prick you if you don't pass this on and the doe
stepped on the pear, they lay on it as if they
would hatch eggs and the marmalade was ready.
But how to get hold of it? Nobody could solve
this. The marmalade rotted in the field as
the boy stared through the window. He was not
questioned. And when he was asked geography
the next day, time was at standstill and he
said: animals, too, are awkward fellows. Next
time, I'll ask my grandpa. Bang! The big
chunk of California tumbled into the sea.

PASTORELA

Swabians have eyes like potatoes. Their mothers
are all waiters. A Jew, okay, but with the dead
mother of art history said Maruška, left and
married in Tübingen. She took with her all my
boxes. Tomorrow is Christmas and I'm
the boy with the bundle. Noble, right? For
the boy with the bundle this was the worst day.
He looked under his skin where there were
nothing but hookers and gave them some
food. *100 hojas de papel bond de primera,*
he copied from his *Scribe* notebook and although
the hookers were slightly consoled he still
didn't know what he should do in the world.
And he took the sea in his hands, looked
if they made a door for him and he clasped it
to his heart. He walked along *calle San Francisco*
and punched a *piñata*, so bonbons were pouring
out. He took a seat on a truck where there
was a live Christmas crib. Jesus was made of
wood, because no mother would give away such
a small boy, but all the others, shepherds, little
angels, Saint Joseph, were his age. They traveled
slowly, people sang and threw oranges from their
windows and still they were supposed to go
to *Plaza de Toros* to climb on the revolvable stage
but it was so windy that they preferred to go home.

THE BIRD DOVE

"La syntaxe est une faculté de l'âme."
But as mine is a glutton, she carries her little
hands in the left palm and eats Huns,
keefeellies and can with a combustible gas
bomb God, eats Vesna, stops above abysses, not
to mention the sprinkling knickers, on her head
she has her limb embittered, an annuity on
a couch and St. Francis's heart, an amber on
all Christ's ringlets, a cubical drudgery,
a forest, a grilled mosquito and Bach, a Venezuela
wreath, three fish on a heap, some of them
not, a cone for a czar's attraction, a male screw
that sleeps in Argentina or on the floor,
the eyes driven by oars, the silence breaking
a steam chest's, with a murnygoonining
of dark powers and knees sprinkled with virgin
spirit's shirts, a power by winch, stars above
horseradish, onion and garlic as Buddha's
lumberjacks, a doe in a musket and Joe on a lake,
bang! silky Kornhauser, and a bystander inside
a Doric moo, one joyful bug, the yellow
spot of the capital on a drying hood and
a sea elephant, a body hair, absolutely adored
other natives don't have it, an earthquake,
tear pearls that grew plants on rock carpets
of all fourteen cathedrals, Ich—goes well
back or in the earth's belly—a closet,
crock, crock on a bear and a lot of meat,
a yodel to kill the streetcar, a hard tiger-like
tribe to soften and stop up the sore uncle,
a poor thing, a damask linen. Veni vidi vici,
spritzee please your coffee in my ear, the dance
danced by Atlas waiting for his satori in front

of the pub, a smell of stupids I like,
herds of deer, not an eyeball, grueling
tunes, no naphthalene, in short, as I slap
God on his little peepers not ever noticing
the rolled up sleeves, my soul thrives, she is
a baroque compass that then collapses so you can
row in peace on the lake and say quietly:

I love you.

TORTURING THE SLAVE

Slave, will your breathing stop?
Or will Slavs ruin their vulva of cabbage.
In the doe's throat is a lacquered ball
eaten by my mom.
Only on it Jerusalem is etched, only on it.
My blotting paper lies in a crystal marsh,
you are guilty, slave!
Look at my optic *garganta*.
Knives gurgling as a water of occult races
untie with the gauze on my finger.
What are you waiting for?
Why can't you stop the weather like
the old highlanders?
They cut down what averted the wind,
snapped at brambles and ground them,
rolling down oak trees.
Wood chutes appeared only later
when gravitation had already won.
You whine 'cause you're soaked, my son,
your calendar is not in the spirit of the Maya,
your hips look stolen from my mountains on
Crete, and when barbarians turn
soil with their boots, you will leave
the revolving door, so
white-hot from loneliness that
the stags will rush into the woods
still smelling of the other burnt doe
and sing the last pious chord of their
suicide.

AMANITA MUSCARIA

An iron collar, different than
a sacred mushroom, strums paths of
technological inventions.
Let us vulcanize claws of the earth's
mind for this
treason.
Cursed be a baboon and this
euphoric asphalt.
He guards the mushroom, he doesn't
eat it. The same rain keeps
falling on the sacred texts, even
if you don't lick honey clean.
Rings are raped.
To encounter the moment
when the world starts to smell life
demands my name.

WARS

After us the Savage God
—W. B. Yeats

Who bowls, bowls
heaven's throne.
A lump of snow as I see it
on the screen is a frozen living spirit.
Are you aware who defined
your life in the war
one against one hundred trillions?
The horse explodes if you
see him through the veil
and a suicide spreads as
the odor of flesh.
Thunderbolt, you, that recoil
from dry ground,
mercenary of god Tezcatlipoca,
you know!
The only soft abyss for
you is my mouth.

EL ÁNGEL EXTERMINADOR

Ángel Exterminador!
I can give you tea!
Ángel Exterminador!
I can give you a book to read!
Ángel Exterminador!
From my window you see
red flowers,
not now!

THE CONFRONTATION

Horn! Silver! Horse!
Horn! Silver! Wind!

Horn! Silver! Sea!
Horn! Silver! Soil!

Horn! Silver! Shadow!
Horn! Silver! Hill!

Horn! Silver! Father!
Horn! Silver! Light!

Horn! Silver! Grass!
Horn! Silver! Brook!

Horn! Silver! Knight!
Horn! Silver! Gift!

Gift!

BY THE DEAD

When comes the time rabbits will be soft
like children hands burnt in concentration camps!

When comes the time suffering will boil
and spill like aura!

When comes the time I will be able to hang on water
and drink it, drink it!

When comes the time of punishment!

When comes the time the mill wheel
will change my bonds to granite dust!

When comes the time my palm will be God!

When comes the time *my* breast will bleed
so palm trees and pine trees and you will grow taller!

When will my soul look at its face!

THERE ARE LITTLE GEESE WE CRACKED THEIR NECKS

but they still live.
Isn't that neat?
There is a mouth gone
but still fragrant.
Isn't this a soul?

Far away,
behind the Hotel Princessa,
a pelican
doesn't see me,
how I march on the beach.

The beam in my sleeping room cracks,
the night is colder than sun.
So I grew up:
from man to mammoth to strange squid
to a grain in the eye—
father cloud hydrogen.

DUOMO

When they gave orders to make me pants for first
communion they cut them as shorts. So I went to
confirmation as a boy scout too. On the way, I kept
killing rats with my keys. I was afraid they would eat my

bike. The door was adorned with flowers. But the watch
deliberately didn't work. They gave us many fancy
cakes and poured the wine on us so that the breath
would not evaporate and escape. There was a gentleman

with a wooden leg creeping around the church. He didn't
look like much. When he flung his wooden leg
into the fountain, the foam sprinkled on those who

brought oranges. Since hosts are flat. Without
the earth light wouldn't exist and steaks would be
flat on the animals who still go baa-aa-h.

SHALL WE GO?

There lived two princesses. One big
and one little. Rivers flowed below them.
Below which one? Below her. And the bread
melted like snow. There lived two birds. One

big and one little. And there was no seed
between the seas and the seas. And the seas
lived one in the other without meeting each
other. There lived two donkeys. One big

and one little. Why do you use the adjective
wrongly? asked the one who knew everything.
To get rid of the saddle. And so he got

everything and princesses' hair, birds' wings
and donkeys' eyes are named after wild
planets we didn't discovered yet, still today.

LAPIS LAZULI

Three nights in a row I spent among gnostics.
White butterflies played tag among red flowers
and snakes turned round to eat themselves.
Here, everything as above. People are

born and die, we lay hands on their heads. Only
my friends' hair was thicker. Will the human
race lose its hair? I've met lynxes telling me
they're from Dacia. There was no Mohammed.

There was a hole in the belly of the earth
because of it. What rotundity! Lumps of
flesh soaked with the spirit and an infinity of
boats with white sails. Do they send off for

oil? Don't think sects were kinder to each other.
Communists swallowed monkeys and monkeys
threw bananas at kings. The pot and the hat
were the same thing. I remember the first night

I cooked meat on a stone, I didn't know
I could use my hat. I've got it!
Our hair lacks grease! Who is still laying
rocks around trunks! The water still rustles

the same while flowing. The skin still beams so
powerful. And the train rushes from the
flesh into the heart and the lizards jumps
from the rails in panic, and the sky is covered

by a scarlet coat . . . No! I say. It's the blue! And I
roll over from on my back to on my belly
and shoot at the sky. And the earth, faces, loves that
passed through my life, all become lapis lazuli.

Do you like kitties more than puppies?
Little dove rests
on Miguel-Angel's hand.

.

Clouds in the sky,
a lamp under a cypress.
My kiss among boats
celebrating the birthday.

.

Lips, come boiling like
crashed rocks, licked to the bottom by the sea.
The sky dances and forgets the dance.

.

We rowed all night to be here now.
The day—where does it spring from—
if not from ourselves?
Leaves are my secret allies.
Everyone falling toward water breathes in the air.

.

What? The whole year and you didn't grow more
body hair? Are you nuts?

.

Look! If I stand like this,
there's Belize.

.

Only if I walk around you
Belize appears to my eyes.

.

I dreamt that I set you on fire in the bush.
First your teeth burnt up,
and, afterwards, your hair.

.

Don't be too cheerful if the people shout with joy.
And don't be too sad if their hearts break.

.

Harriet calls London and says:
Granny! Do you still have cramps in your belly
at the thought you may die before I return?
We cooked the turkey.

.

The Chinaman says: not cooked, grilled.
And I said: not thound, found

EL PARAISO

ACKNOWLEDGEMENTS

The poems listed below previously appeared in the publications indicated.

Bateau: No Jokes in Love; Corrida Comida; Toof, Toof: Arc; Tsar Nikolaj
Bestoned: Opus; I'm cursed.; The deer's face; The arm that walks
Denver Quarterly: The Phoenicians; Northern Seas; The Boy with the Small Bundle
Fence: Seed
Forklift: Sierra Nevada
Hinchas de Poesia: El Grito; To Deaf Brothers
Island: Christ; Pastorela
Jubilat: For David, God from the Eighth Floor
Kenyon Review: Prayer for Bread
Lana Turner: To the Heart
Locutio: Querétaro; Robi; The Little Man; The Name of the World, The Bird Dove
Mead: They All; Poppy
Nimrod: They All; Poppy; Full Moon
Paperbag: Cantina in Querétaro; About the Mouth of a River; December 8, 1980, 170 Years after Gérard de Nerval's Mother's Death; Torturing the Slave
Poem: Nihil est in intelectu...; Tsar Nikolaj
Poetry International: El Angel Exterminador
Rialto: Death's Window, The Turtle
Shing Wang: Opus; For David; I'm cursed.; The deer's face; The arm that walks, kneels and jumps
Shoppinghour: The Sky Above Querétaro
Sol: The Kiss Across the Ocean; The Morning; About Heaven and Earth
Stand: To Deaf Brothers; Cantina in Querétaro
Taos: Amanita Muscaria; Wars
Transom: The Aztec; Evening Among Muses; By the Dead; Duomo
Washingtom Square: Shall We Go?
Wolf: The Aztec

MICHAL AJVAZ, *The Golden Age.*
The Other City.

PIERRE ALBERT-BIROT, *Grabinoulor.*

YUZ ALESHKOVSKY, *Kangaroo.*

FELIPE ALFAU, *Chromos.*
Locos.

IVAN ÂNGELO, *The Celebration.*
The Tower of Glass.

ANTÓNIO LOBO ANTUNES,
Knowledge of Hell.
The Splendor of Portugal.

ALAIN MRIAS-MISSON, *Theatre of Incest.*

JOHN ASHBERY AND JAMES SCHUYLER,
A Nest of Ninnies.

ROBERT ASHLEY, *Perfect Lives.*

GABRIELA AVIGUR-ROTEM,
Heatwave and Crazy Birds.

DJUNA BARNES, *Ladies Almanack.*
Ryder.

JOHN BARTH, *Letters.*
Sabbatical.

DONALD BARTHELME, *The King.*
Paradise.

SVETISLAV BASARA, *Chinese Letter.*

MIQUEL BAUÇÀ, *The Siege in the Room.*

RENÉ BELLETTO, *Dying.*

MAREK BIEŃCZYK, *Transparency.*

ANDREI BITOV, *Pushkin House.*

ANDREJ BLATNIK, *You Do Understand.*

LOUIS PAUL BOON, *Chapel Road.*
My Little War.
Summer in Termuren.

ROGER BOYLAN, *Killoyle.*

IGNÁCIO DE LOYOLA BRANDÃO,
Anonymous Celebrity.
Zero.

BONNIE BREMSER, *Troia: Mexican Memoirs.*

CHRISTINE BROOKE-ROSE,
Amalgamemnon.

BRIGID BROPHY, *In Transit.*

GERALD L. BRUNS,
Modern Poetry and the Idea of Language.

GABRIELLE BURTON, *Heartbreak Hotel.*

MICHEL BUTOR, *Degrees,*
Mobile.

G. CABRERA INFANTE,
Infante's Inferno.
Three Trapped Tigers.

JULIETA CAMPMPOS,
The Fear of Losing Eurydice.

ANNE CARSON, *Eros the Bittersweet.*

ORLY CASTEL-BLOOM, *Dolly City.*

LOUIS-FERDINAND CÉLINE,
Castle to Castle.
Conversations with Professor Y,
London Bridge,
Normance,
North,
Rigadoon.

MARIE CHAIX,
The Laurels of Lake Constance.

HUGO CHARTERIS, *The Tide Is Right.*

ERIC CHEVILLARD, *Demolishing Nisard.*

MARC CHOLODENKO, *Mordechai Schamz.*

JOSHUA COHEN, *Witz.*

EMILY HOLMES COLEMAN,
The Shutter of Snow.

ROBERT COOVER, *A Night at the Movies.*

STANLEY CRAWFORD, *Log of the S.S,*
The Mrs Unguentine,
Some Instructions to My Wife.

RENÉ CREVEL, PUTTING *My Foot in It.*

RALPH CUSACK, *Cadenza.*

NICHOLAS DELBANCO,
The Count of Concord,
Sherbrookes.

NIGEL DENNIS, *Cards of Identity.*

PETER DIMOCK,
A Short Rhetoric for Leaving the Family.

ARIEL DORFMFMAN, *Konfidenz.*

AIDAN HIGGINS, *Balcony of Europe,*
  Blind Man's Bluff,
  Bornholm Night-Ferry,
  Flotsam and Jetsam,
  Langrishe, Go Down,
  Scenes from a Receding Past.

KEIZO HINO, *Isle of Dreams.*

KAZUSHI HOSAKA, *Plainsong.*

ALDOUS HUXLEY, *Antic Hay,*
  Crome Yellow,
  Point Counter Point,
  Those Barren Leaves,
  Time Must Have a Stop.

NAOYUKI II, *The Shadow of a Blue Cat.*

GERT JONKE, *The Distant Sound,*
  Geometric Regional Novel,
  Homage to Czerny,
  The System of Vienna.

JACQUES JOUET, *Mountain R,*
  Savage,
  Upstaged.

MIEKO KANAI, *The Word Book.*

YORAM KANIUK, *Life on Sandpaper.*

HUGH KENNER, Flaubert,
  Joyce and Beckett: The Stoic Comedians,
  Joyce's Voices.

DANILO KIS̆, *The Attic,*
  Garden, Ashes,
  The Lute and the Scars,
  Psalm 44,
  A Tomb for Boris Davidovich.

ANITA KONKKA, *A Fool's Paradise.*

GEORGE KONRÁD, *The City Builder.*

TADEUSZ KONWICKI,
  A Minor Apocalypse,
  The Polish Complex.

MENIS KOUMANDAREAS, *Koula.*

ELAINE KRAF, *The Princess of 72nd Street.*

JIM KRUSOE, *Iceland.*

AYŞE KULIN,
  Farewell: A Mansion in Occupied Istanbul.

EMILIO LASCANO TEGUI,
  On Elegance While Sleeping.

ERIC LAURRENT, *Do Not Touch.*

VIOLETTE LEDUC, *La Bâtarde.*

EDOUARD LEVÉ, *Autoportrait,*
  Suicide.

MARIO LEVI, *Istanbul Was a Fairy Tale.*

DEBORAH LEVY, *Billy and Girl.*

JOSE´ LEZAMA LIMA, *Paradiso.*

ROSA LIKSOM, *Dark Paradise.*

OSMAN LINS,
  Avalovara,
  The Queen of the Prisons of Greece.

ALF MAC LOCHLAINN,
  The Corpus in the Library,
  Out of Focus.

RON LOEWINSOHN, *Magnetic Field(s).*

MINA LOY, *Stories and Essays of Mina Loy.*

D. KEITH MANO, *Take Five.*

MICHELINE AHARONIAN MARCOM,
  The Mirror in the Well.

BEN MARCUS, *The Age of Wire and String.*

WALLACE MARKFIELD, *Teitlebaum's*
  Window,
  To an Early Grave.

DAVID MARKSON, *Reader's Block,*
  Wittgenstein's Mistress.

CAROLE MASO, *AVA.*

LADISLAV MATEJKA &
KRYSTYNA POMORSKA, EDS.,
  Readings in Russian Poetics: Formalist and
  Structuralist Views.

HARRY MATHEWS, *Cigarettes,*
  The Conversions,
  The Human Country: New and Collected Stories,
  The Journalist,
  My Life in CIA,
  Singular Pleasures,
  The Sinking of the Odradek
  Stadium,
  Tlooth.

JOSEPH MCELROY,
  Night Soul and Other Stories.

FOR A FULL LIST OF PUBLICATIONS, VISIT: www.dalkeyarchive.com

ABDELWAHAB MEDDEB, *Talismano.*

GERHARD MEIER, *Isle of the Dead.*

HERMAN MELVILLE, *The Confidence-Man.*

AMANDA MICHALOPOULOU, *I'd Like.*

STEVEN MILLHAUSER,
  The Barnum Museum,
  In the Penny Arcade.

RALPH J. MILLS, JR., *Essays on Poetry.*

MOMUS, *The Book of Jokes.*

CHRISTINE MONTALBETTI,
  The Origin of Man,
  Western.

OLIVE MOORE, *Spleen.*

NICHOLAS MOSLEY, *Accident,*
  Assassins,
  Catastrophe Practice,
  Experience and Religion,
  A Garden of Trees,
  Hopeful Monsters,
  Imago Bird,
  Impossible Object,
  Inventing God,
  Judith,
  Look at the Dark,
  Natalie Natalia,
  Serpent,
  Time at War.

WARREN MOTTE, *Fables of the Novel: French Fiction since 1990,*
  Fiction Now: The French Novel in the 21st Century,
  Oulipo: A Primer of Potential Literature.

GERALD MURNANE, *Barley Patch,*
  Inland.

YVES NAVARRE,
  Our Share of Time,
  Sweet Tooth.

DOROTHY NELSON, *In Night's City,*
  Tar and Feathers.

ESHKOL NEVO, *Homesick.*

WILFRIDO D D. NOLLEDO,
  But for the Lovers.

FLANN O'BRIEN, *At Swim-Two-Birds,*
  The Best of Myles,
  The Dalkey Archive,
  The Hard Life,
  The Poor Mouth,
  The Third Policeman.

CLAUDE OLLIER, *The Mise-en-Scène,*
  Wert and the Life Without End.

GIOVANNI ORELLI, *Walaschek's Dream.*

PATRIK OUŘEDNÍK, *Europeana,*
  The Opportune Moment, 1855.

BORIS PAHOR, *Necropolis.*

FERNANDO DEL PASO,
  News from the Empire,
  Palinuro of Mexico.

ROBERT PINGET, *The Inquisitory,*
  Mahu or The Material,
  Trio.

MANUEL PUIG, *Betrayed by Rita Hayworth,*
  The Buenos Aires Affair,
  Heartbreak Tango.

RAYMYMOND QUENEAU, *The Last Days,*
  Odile,
  Pierrot Mon Ami,
  Saint Glinglin.

ANN QUIN, *Berg,*
  Passages,
  Three,
  Tripticks.

ISHMAEL REED, *The Free-Lance Pallbearers,*
  The Last Days of Louisiana Red,
  Ishmael Reed: The Plays,
  Juice!,
  Reckless Eyeballing,
  The Terrible Threes,
  The Terrible Twos,
  Yellow Back Radio Broke-Down.

JASIA REICHARDT,
  15 Journeys Warsaw to London.

NOËLLE REVAZ,
  With the Animals.

JOÃO UBALDO RIBEIRO,
  House of the Fortunate Buddhas.

JEAN RICARDOU, *Place Names*.

RAINER MARIA RILKE,
The Notebooks of Malte Laurids Brigge.

JULIÁN RÍOS, *The House of Ulysses*,
Larva: A Midsummer Night's Babel,
Poundemonium,
Procession of Shadows.

AUGUSTO ROA BASTOS, *I the Supreme*.

DANIËL ROBBERECHTS,
Arriving in Avignon.

JEAN ROLIN,
The Explosion of the Radiator Hose.

OLIVIER ROLIN, *Hotel Crystal*.

ALIX CLEO ROUBAUD, *Alix's Journal*.

JACQUES ROUBAUD,
The Form of a City Changes Faster, Alas,
Than the Human Heart,
The Great Fire of London,
Hortense in Exile,
Hortense Is Abducted,
The Loop,
Mathematics, The Plurality of Worlds of Lewis,
The Princess Hoppy,
Some Thing Black.

RAYMYMOND ROUSSEL,
Impressions of Africa.

VEDRANA RUDAN, *Night*.

STIG SÆTERBAKKEN, *Siamese, Self Control*.

LYDIE SALVAYRE, *The Company of Ghosts*,
The Lecture,
The Power of Flies.

LUIS RAFAEL SÁNCHEZ,
Macho Camacho's Beat.

SEVERO SARDUY, *Cobra & Maitreya*.

NATHALIE SARRAUTE,
Do You Hear Them?,
Martereau,
The Planetarium.

ARNO SCHMIDT, *Collected Novellas*,
Collected Stories,
Nobodaddy's Children,
Two Novels.

ASAF SCHURR, *Motti*.

GAIL SCOTT, *My Paris*.

DAMION SEARLS, *What We Were Doing and*
Where We Were Going.

JUNE AKERS SEESE,
Is This What Other Women Feel Too?,
What Waiting Really Means.

BERNARD SHARE, *Inish, Transit*.

VIKTOR SHKLOVSKY, *Bowstring*,
Knight's Move,
A Sentimental Journey: Memoirs 1917–1922,
Energy of Delusion: A Book on Plot,
Literature and Cinematography,
Theory of Prose,
Third Factory,
Zoo, or Letters Not about Love.

PIERRE SINIAC, *The Collaborators*.

KJERSTI A. SKOMSVOLD,
The Faster I Walk, the Smaller I Am.

JOSEF SˇKVORECKYˊ,
The Engineer of Human Souls.

GILBERT SORRENTINO,
Aberration of Starlight,
Blue Pastoral,
Crystal Vision,
Imaginative Qualities of Actual Things,
Mulligan Stew,
Pack of Lies,
Red the Fiend,
The Sky Changes,
Something Said,
Splendide-Hôtel,
Steelwork,
Under the Shadow.

W. M. SPACKMAN, *The Complete Fiction*.

ANDRZEJ STASIUK, *Dukla*,
Fado.

GERTRUDE STEIN, *The Making of Americans*,
A Novel of Thank You.

LARS SVENDSEN, *A Philosophy of Evil*.

PIOTR SZEWC, *Annihilation*.

GONÇALO M. TAVARES, *Jerusalem*,
Joseph Walser's Machine,
Learning to Pray in the Age of Technique.

⊡ SELECTED DALKEY ARCHIVE TITLES